Published by TechWrite! Publishing
Atlanta, GA

For the Tech Hobbyist:

Home server components – A quick overview

Foreword

The first book in this series introduced you to the idea of building your server. It covered the reasons to have a server at home, what a home server can do and it also had a brief introduction about the types of hardware that you could choose from.

This is the second book in the series. It is a somewhat deeper dive into the hardware that will serve you best over the long haul. I include very little specific hardware manufacturer information, the goal here is to provide concepts and planning ideas, not manufacturer blurbs. In the time that I've experimented with computer hardware I've discovered that just because a brand has a huge market share, it's no guarantee of quality. Components that have been purchased from major vendors have died moments after being turned on for the first time and even right out of the box once or twice. I've also found that sometimes the little guys can surprise you with how sturdy their equipment can be, so try not to get locked into thinking of one 'camp' or the other. You want to keep an open mind when you're experimenting because it helps you pick what's best for you, not the best for some conglomerate. Remember, it's very important to do good research before you buy anything. If you're going to use hardware you already have lying around, do research on that. 10 or 15 minutes' (or more) worth of research can save you hours of rework time when something doesn't work properly the first time. Learn what you can before you start, that always makes things easier in the long run.

Although I will be covering server hardware please understand that this series of books is intended for those of us who like to experiment with computers and software. These books don't have the depth you would require to do things like become a Systems Administrator or Server Engineer. I stop the instruction level at basic configuration. If you are considering a career in Information Technology realize that the level of education you will get from experimenting just scratches the surface of how much work goes into building a true knowledgebase of information technology subject matter. Don't get me wrong, experimenting is a great place to start, but following the steps in this book series is not enough to help you qualify for getting a job.

Having said that let me add that one of the true marks of a lifelong IT Specialist is the desire to learn how technology works and then to find ways to incorporate that knowledge into your life. Deep inside you want to KNOW. You want to find ways to do things that haven't been done before or discover a new way to do something old. This more than *anything* else forms the core of an IT career. And even if you don't want to work exclusively in technology, learning these skills will help you in other aspects of life. Computers, servers, networks, and the offshoots they spawn are here to stay. They are already an integrated part of any business you might ever be involved with – I don't care if you work in a flower shop, a hospital, as an auto mechanic or a dog groomer – there's a computer involved somewhere. At this point computer literacy should be second nature.

For my own part I did this all of this for free for years out of sheer love of computer systems. I fixed computers for family and friends and did my happy dance every time I built a new system and it worked properly. That's the essence of being a hobbyist. These books are for others who love this stuff as much as I do.

About For the Tech Hobbyist

This series of books has grown out of my passion to learn about technology and then finding ways to make what I learn work for me at home or in my businesses. I've been involved in IT professionally and as an adherent for over 20 years and though I don't know probably half as much as I should, it's the love of the process (building, learning reading, talking to other technologists, coming up with new ideas and being excited when things work) that keeps me coming back for more. There is nothing like building a machine with your hands and your brain, turning it on and watching it do something amazing.

It's my greatest hope that you will glean some useful information from this book series and that my love of technology and the process sings to you on some level to ignite your creative spark.

Good luck on the journey!

What you will learn in this book?

- An overview of the major components you will need to build a solid machine
  - o Individual component information
  - o Is there really a difference between 'brands'?
- More explanation about 32 vs 64 bit hardware
  - o What it is
  - o Why is this important to you as a hobbyist
- Basic configurations
  - o To RAID or not to RAID
  - o Motherboard
  - o Hard drive
  - o RAM
  - o Processor
  - o A few things to keep in mind when building from scratch
  - o A few things to keep in mind when re-purposing components

With that in mind, let's get started!

Table of Contents

Part 1 – Components

It doesn't take a very long time to design and build a server. I know that sounds a little funny right now because you haven't actually built anything, but trust me, all of the planning needed to build a server that will last you many years can be accomplished in an afternoon.

The first thing to remember is that you should have a solid idea what you want to do with the server. Is it going to store files for later retrieval? Is it going to stream media to every point of your home? Is it going to allow you to show off your web design skills to the world?

Your answers to these questions will drive the choices you make for hardware. If you need a machine that's going to run 24/7 you will most likely need a different processor and power supply from a machine that will only be on a few hours each day. If you just to back up your home PC's and the machine will never receive a client request you won't need massive amounts of RAM, but you will need the largest hard drives you can afford. There are times when being able to save money on component A will allow you to purchase a better quality component B. Saving money and potentially time on any system build is important.

Okay, let's look at the basic components that make up a server.

Any server is comprised of the following parts -

- Case
- Motherboard
- Power supply
- Memory
- Hard Drive(s)
- Processor(s)

Case

The case is one of the more flexible choices you can make. They range in size from 17 or 18 inches high and 6 inches wide to 20 or 24 inches high and 6 to 8 inches wide. There are good and bad points to the size issue with cases. Smaller cases limit the number of hard drives, the amount of RAM, the type of hard drive and other devices you can install. Larger cases can allow more hard drives, more cooling fans and other components into the machine with the flip side being extra weight, more power consumption and heat being produced going up very quickly. There are 'mini-ATX' cases, 'full tower' cases and 'rack mountable' cases. Some of the choice for a case is aesthetic, but never sacrifice functionality and expandability for looks. Remember, for the most part this machine will be sitting in a closet somewhere quietly minding its own business.

Also, and this point alone could make your choice all by itself - larger cases aren't always the best choice despite having multiple bays and plenty of room for your hands. With the advent of multi-terabyte hard drives and old standby's like mini-ATX boards, low profile expansion cards and memory, you can get as much use out of a smaller case as a larger one.

Motherboard

I'm building a bit of a fudge factor into this section because realistically you should be looking at server motherboards instead of standard desktop PC motherboards. However, since you're building for home and not a production environment you probably won't need a board with 3 processor slots and 8 memory ports and enough expansion slots to start your own parts sales company.

That said, many board manufacturers are coming around to the notion that there's a growing market of home server and small business builders. So with careful research you can definitely find some great deals out there for a server grade motherboard that won't break the bank.

First I'll point out a few basics and then we can get into the meat of the thing.

Motherboards are –
- The central connecting point for every internal component inside the case and there is also an input/output port on one side that allowed devices to be plugged into the motherboard once the machine is built
- The device that determines things like
  - The amount of RAM that can be physically installed.
  - What speed the data buses run. (*buses are connections between components inside the case that handle data transfer between the device and the computer*)
  - What type of processor will fit. (*the processor sits in a special port called a socket*)
  - What form factor the machine will be, which gives you some flexibility in what size case to use.

The difference between a server motherboard and a PC motherboard can be significant. There are several factors including bus speed, amount and type of RAM you can use, dual or sometimes more processor sockets, additional expansion card slots, additional SATA slots for running multiple hard drives, specialized heat sinks that are designed to wick heat away from the more tender bits and other components that you won't find in on a desktop PC motherboard.

Server motherboards are designed this way because a server tends to have a greater load put upon it and needs to be a solid, dependable machine for years at a stretch. I know of servers that have been sitting on racks running non-stop (*with obvious maintenance of course*) for as long as 8 to 10 years.

When you start doing your research its important to understand that the motherboard is frequently overlooked in its importance. The processor has the 'ohh shiny' factor going for it, but the motherboard does the lion's share of work where dependable machine operation is concerned. Motherboards are exposed to heat, dust, constant noise and vibration from components inside the case. The board itself is made of fiberglass and though they are usually tough as nails, they can also be amazingly fragile.

Compare a few models side by side. Check out the specs and pay close attention to things like how does the board handle power from the power supply (*how many power ports are there, where is the 4 pin port, are the fan power plugs going to sit under the hard drive bay*), how many memory ports are there and how are they positioned, how many SATA ports are there, does the board look fairly easy to manipulate once you start adding components (*you'd be surprised how fast you run out of finger room…*), and pay close attention to where the processor sockets are located. This, more than anything else, can cause big problems when putting the unit together. I have seen many units that put the RAM ports in a position that you can no longer reach them once the board and processor fan or the system power cables are installed in the case. The best alignment for the processor socket is somewhere near the middle of the board. If the socket is too close to one edge or two close to the RAM ports you might have problems.

Power Supplies

The power supply is another of the more flexible components. Power supplies are rated in wattage. Depending on the components you want to run you'll use one rated between 300 and potentially as high as 800 watts. More than that and you will definitely notice a bump in your electric usage. Its always best to buy a unit rated slightly above what you think you might need.

As an example, say you are running a basic server with an Intel processor (more on this later), 8 GB of memory, and 4 TB of hard drive space. There's no need for a video card, audio card or optical drive since you'll be doing the operating system install via flash drive. With that format you'd only need a 200 watt power supply (not that you can find one that small anymore, this is just to illustrate my point). Even if you fully loaded the box with the other things I left out, you wouldn't need more than a 450 watt supply.

If you want to get an idea how these calculations work run a search for 'calculating power supply wattage' on the web. There are dozens of sites with calculators for you to choose from.

As with everything else, the higher the wattage the more expensive the unit. The larger issue you'll want to get details on are the number of SATA cables (*used to connect hard drives to the motherboard*), Molex connectors (*used to connect power to various devices like the motherboard, CD/DVD drives, and older hard drive inside the case*) and other peripheral cables (*used to connect things like fans, lights, and USB ports*) the power supply can support. The more cables the supply has, the more components you can support.

Memory

Before I begin this section I think I should take a minute to explain how memory works in a server, it's a little bit different than how it works in a pc. In a nutshell there are two types of memory, error correcting code (ECC) and non-error correcting code (non-ECC). ECC memory works to test and correct any memory errors that it comes across. What this basically means is the correcting feature acts as a safety valve to keep the processor working properly. The processor receives its instructions from memory and if those instructions are inaccurate or otherwise corrupted the processor will deliver incorrect results to the system and therefore the user. Perhaps you've seen the memory error screens pop-up on your computer from time to time usually followed by the computer freezing or even crashing – this is where problems like that usually begin.

Since servers are responsible for storing data and then serving that data to the client PC's when requested or sometimes providing access to running applications, you want the best possible type and amount of memory on the case. 'Regular' computers can use ECC memory, but usually it's not necessary since they are only responsible for running their own software. The second part of the equation is the amount of memory that you have working on the system. The amount of memory that you have available for use will be a huge factor in how well the server works for you. With a machine that's expected to act as a server you want to have a minimum of 8 GB with 24 or 32 GB being the 'usual' maximums. Again, it's all about what you plan to do with the machine. A streaming media server will be fine with 6 or 8 GB of memory while a backup server, busy web server or application server wouldn't be worth building with less than 24 GB. I have a physical machine acting as a secondary network attached storage (NAS) that's running fine with 6 GB of RAM, but the only reason that works is because I'm the only one who currently uses it. If I added additional users (and therefore workload) to the machine I would have to bump up the RAM considerably or the performance would suffer.

RAM serves a few functions in a server, it allows faster opening and closing of applications, it allows more accurate processing to take place and it also allows for more applications to run at the same time. As an example of the last statement let's take a quick look at my primary virtual server.

When I first built it, the machine had 12 GB of RAM. I'm running an operating system called VMWare ESXi (there will be much more on the Operating systems in book 3 of this series). The OS allows me to create multiple virtual machines on a single hard drive and as far as the hardware is concerned each one of the 'virtual' machines is a real living, breathing computer. The thing that allows me to run more than one of these computers at the same time is memory. I'll cover this more in a later book, but when you create a virtual machine one of the creation steps is to give it a certain amount of memory to run with. The memory that the machine uses comes from the total RAM in the physical machine. It's simple math. With 12 GB of memory I could open and run three 4 GB 'servers' or four 3 GB machines.

Understand how it works?

Of course the more memory, the better. Right now the original virtual host (the physical server) I mentioned now has 32 GB of RAM installed. As a result I can now open and simultaneously run up to eight 4 GB servers at the same time before I start running into problems with slowdowns with the physical machine. (There's a bit of a fudge factor in there because the physical server also requires RAM to run, but I'm just illustrating a point. Depending on the operating system you pick, 4 GB of RAM for the virtual machine might be overkill.)

As you can see, this segment is getting pretty long and I've really just scratched the surface where memory is concerned. There's enough information out there to fill a book all by itself. Hmm, come to think of it, maybe I'll write one...

I'm also hoping that you can see the importance of this component because of how much time I gave it. This is one area where it doesn't pay to scrimp. Do your research carefully!

Hard Drives (or more accurately – Storage)

I'm calling this segment hard drives, mostly out of habit and mostly because what you'll be buying or repurposing will BE a hard drive. But here's the issue – when you build a server it's not really about the 'hard drives', it's about way you want to configure your storage. It can be daunting because there are so many formats out there. Should you pick SATA or eSATA? Should you go with solid state drives or traditional spinning drives? Are the prices for 2 TB drives better this week than they were last month? How many drives should you purchase and how should you put them together (I'll cover RAID in just a little bit) to give yourself the best performance at a decent price (and hopefully LONG service)?

Lots of questions, let's see if we can answer a few of them.

Your server, no matter what type you build, is going to require storage. If you're building a machine intended as a backup server, or a streaming media device, or a rendering server it's going to require a LOT of storage. The first thing to think about is of course reliability. There is nothing worse than putting a bunch of your favorite files onto a hard drive and for that hard drive to then fail.

Every company that sells storage solutions has a vested interest in keeping their customers happy. As a result almost all of them feature spec pages for their drives that detail things like speed and heat ratings, operating power requirements, the onboard memory cache (how much internal memory the hard drive has), and even the specific type of operating system the device is capable of running. If you are buying a new hard drive these specification pages are where you want to begin. To my way of thinking this information is almost more important than the price.

Here are a few definitions that will help –

- SATA or Serial ATA – The current standard hardware interface for connecting hard drives, solid state drives (SSDs) and CD/DVD drives to the computer.
- SCSI or Small Computer System Interface – a hardware interface for up to 15 peripherals connected to one PCI or PCI Express card on the motherboard.
- eSATA – refers to ports on the motherboard (or back of the computer) that accept external SATA drives. So the drives are basically the same, they just connect differently.
- SSD or Solid State Drives – A hard drive that employs the same technology that is found in flash drives or thumb drives. The term solid state comes from the fact that the drive does not have spinning platters in it. A benefit to not having moving parts is a serious increase in seek speeds; there are no heads to move around looking for data. Another benefit of having no moving parts is that these drives are generally more reliable than standard hard drives, there are no motors to fail or platters to wear out. There is one serious drawback though, these type drives are much more expensive per gigabyte than standard drives. That is changing, but it will be a while before the prices are comparable.
- Gigabyte vs Terabyte – I won't go too deep into this one, but a quick refresher is probably in order, here are the basics:
  - A gigabyte (GB) is 1 billion bytes and can store
    - Just under 19,000 word docs
    - One hour of video
    - About 230 songs, right around 16 hours of music
    - Between 250 and 340 images (depending on quality)
  - A terabyte (TB) is 1,000 gigabytes and can store
    - An estimated 85,899,345 word document pages (no one has actually attempted this that I know of...)

- About 250 2 hour movies
- About 17,000 hours of music (200,000 or so songs)
- About 300,000 images (again, depending on the quality)
  - All of these amounts are based on 'average' file sizes
    - Documents – 50 KB
    - Images – 2 MB
    - Movies – 1 to 1.5 GB
    - Music – 4 MB

Depending on what you're building and/or how it's going to be used, hard drives are another of the more 'flexible' choices. Size and brand are totally dependent on your current and future needs. The results of the research you do will definitely turn you one way or another. Servers that aren't intended to store large amounts of data or servers that use external storage sources really don't need multiple terabytes of space. Also, there is a noticeable variation in price depending on the size and brand that you choose. The key here is to think in terms of initial cost, system requirements and future expansion.

- Are you backing up multiple computers? Will that number grow over time?
- Will you be adding more users internally or externally?
- Are you expecting to have to scale up storage for a small business?
- If you are collecting movies or family photos and personal video you will run out of storage space much faster than it seems you would (this is one the things I experienced that surprised me).
- As your skill and experience grow you will undoubtedly want to build bigger and better machines, or expand/update ones you've already built.

You might start out just building a server for fun, but as I've said, once this stuff gets in your blood it's hard to turn off...

A brief segue into RAID

The concept of RAID is one of those 'so simple it's complicated' subjects. The letters used to stand for *Redundant Array of Inexpensive Disks*, but it is more common now to refer to it as a *Redundant Array of Independent Disks*. At its core RAID is a data storage technology (*it can be either hardware or software based*) that turns a number of hard drives into a 'single logical drive'. The concept is pretty simple; it works on the principle of 'the sum is greater than its parts'. Here are some reasons to consider RAID when building your server:

- Provides data redundancy because the bits are written across multiple disks. Depending on the format you use, you can lose one or two drives and still not lose any data.
- Performance improvement – this is another benefit of multiple drives. Because the data is written across multiple disks things can be set up in a way that speeds up searches and data access
- Increased fault tolerance – this one comes from the fact that the drives probably don't all have the same manufacture date or even brand name. Any hard drive has a 'work life' that is commonly known as a mean time between failures (MTBF) which is the amount of hours that a spinning platter drive will work before it dies. Even solid state drives do eventually fail although the reason typically isn't the same as a drive with motors, spinning heads and moving armatures. Since the drives have different MTBF's having multiple drives fail at the same time is exceedingly rare which gives you a level of security that running with one drive can't.

- There are multiple RAID levels that perform the data storage function differently. Each has its strengths, weaknesses and best use cases.

There are about a billion places on the web that explain RAID and there's also a For the Tech Hobbyist book in the works that covers RAID in more detail. I suggest adding some online reading to your research. This is a pretty deep subject and well worth your time to learn more about.

Processors

The central processing unit (CPU) or more commonly – processor – is the center of the system.

It is the 'brain' that crunches numbers, performs operations and centralizes almost all of the other functions that go on while the server is doing its thing. At the core what a processor does is accept the input of digital or binary data from the applications running in RAM or from the hard wired components on the motherboard (*everything inside the box has to play nice or its game over*). It interprets the data it received and then it performs calculations on that data. When it finishes the calculations it outputs the results to you in a form you can see, hear or touch and it also instructs the system peripherals of any tasks they must do with the results. IE – print something, draw something, send something, receive something, block something...you get the idea.

To be clear, I am skipping over a whole host of things that are really going on, but I'm not trying to put you to sleep and the minutia really isn't applicable to what I'm saying here.

Your primary concern with processors is the speed at which they're running (*the clock speed, measured in gigahertz (GHz) refers to the number of instructions the processor is running - 3.0 Ghz means over 3 billion instructions per second*), the number of 'cores' (*multiple processing units squeezed onto the same chip*), and depending on what you're building, whether it's 32 or 64 bit.

This is a good place to stop and talk about why 32 vs 64 bit matters.

First this list –

- 64 bit processors can have multiple cores (dual, quad, six, and eight core) allowing for a larger number of calculations per second, thus the system is faster
- 64 bit processors can handle RAM above 4 GB in size (into the Terabyte range if necessary)
- 64 bit processors (with the proper extensions enabled) can run virtualization software/virtual machines
- 32 bit processors have either single, dual or quad cores only
- 32 bit processors can handle a maximum of 4 GB of RAM (or slightly less depending on the operating system you use. There is a way to support more physical RAM, but its outside the scope of this book and it also doesn't change the amount of virtual address space that's available)
- 32 bit processors cannot natively run virtual machines, however its best to check in your BIOS to see if the processor is secretly a 64 bit capable device and that it has the proper virtual extensions that you can turn on. The best program I've seen to check whether or not your machine is capable is CPU-Z at www.cpuid.com although Belarc is much more detailed. You can find Belarc at http://www.belarc.com/free_download.html .

Here's the return from CPU-Z for the machine I'm writing this book on –

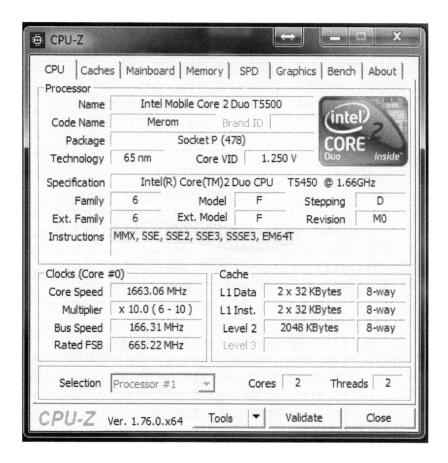

No virtual instructions (VT-x or AMD-V, there are others but don't worry about that for now) appear in that box, this machine would not be able to run VM's.

So what does it all mean?

In a nutshell the terms 32-bit and 64-bit refer to the way a computer's processor handles information.

64 bit machines are capable of handling much larger amounts of RAM than 32 bit machines. If the processor has multiple cores it is also capable of running calculations faster, make the machine itself faster. Even though 64 bit is essentially the

'future' of computing that doesn't mean that you should ignore re-purposing an existing 32 bit system. As I said in the first book, one of my original servers is an ancient WinbookXL (*look that one up if you need a hearty belly laugh...*). That machine serves its purpose just fine. I only mention the differences as a way to illustrate the types of systems that are available and demonstrate how they play a role in your choices.

Okay, back to Processors!

The processor does all of the heavy lifting in the operation of your server. It is arguably the most important component in the whole mix. Without it you don't really have a server. You can get by with an external power source, minimal RAM and even a 32 GB flash drive as your storage device, but the processor isn't somewhere to skimp. If you have to buy one look for the best deal you can find. Average speeds have been between 2.6 GHz and 3.5 GHz for several years now. You can buy units on either side of those numbers but go too low and you will lose out on performance, go too high and you'll either spend too much money or end up with a unit that eats power and requires a city sized water tower to cool. Remember, you're not building a hot rod, you're building a quarter horse. The only time speed REALLY matters with a server is when you are sending requests to it and when it is responding, otherwise the unit is more or less idle.

Section Summary

It's important to mention that the information I've given above is focused on using off the shelf computer components or re-purposing systems you already have to build home servers. I have ignored 'actual server' hardware on purpose. Most items that are designed for servers are very expensive and probably more powerful than you would need as a hobbyist. For example, a 2 TB internal hard drive would run you between $50 and $100. A similar 2 TB hard SAS drive meant for use in a server would start at close to $200 and go up from there. The higher end stuff also adds a level of complexity to your build that would ultimately take a lot of the fun out of the whole thing. Let the enterprise level guys worry about that stuff, you're just trying to have fun and build something cool!

Unless you are after a very specific set of goals with your server there's no need to spend the higher prices when you can get the same performance from less costly hardware.

Part 2 – Getting picky with it

- Comparisons
- More memory or less memory
- External Storage vs network storage vs internal storage
- To RAID or not to RAID
- Section Summary

Comparisons

As I said, I'm not going to talk about one brand over the other. I don't really care what brand you get so long as you do your homework before spending a dime.

What I want to talk about here is the concept of performing your own side by side comparisons. Never jump at the first deal that looks good or costs the cheapest, there's no need to rush into it, you're doing this for fun so taking your time just enhances the anticipation. What I suggest is when you go to your favorite retailer website (or wholesaler if you have access to a reputable one) run a search for the component you want and then do some serious horse trading. Look at the spec sheet if one is available. Compare two brands or two models side by side if you can, look for glaring inconsistencies. It doesn't matter if you've never done this before, I'm betting that your smart enough to notice a problem when a manufacturer or website promises a 100 year run time on a hard drive that they're only asking $25 for.

What you're doing here is familiarizing yourself with individual component specifications. Look at how they're written up, compare the size, speed, wattage, cooling capability, special system needs, power consumption, etc. TAKE GOOD NOTES!!

Full disclosure – I have spent hours comparing parts because I'm that type (*and I procrastinate a lot...*) but it has always paid off in the end. I have rarely ordered something only to have to send it back because it was incorrect for my needs.

Once you are satisfied that you have all of the info you need break out your server planning notes and compare the two. Did you remember to get enough memory? How about that hard drive? Did you have to cut a corner somewhere out of financial need? If so, can you still make your idea work with what you researched? Probably, but double checking is never a bad idea.

More memory or less memory

Sometimes you find that you can get away with less memory, at least initially. One of my FreeNAS servers is running with only 6 GB of RAM. FreeNAS recommends a minimum of 8, but the system works for me because right now I'm the only one using it. When it comes time to build an FTP connection to that box, make it available online and add 4 other users I'm going to have to upgrade the RAM what they specify or even more.

I say this to illustrate the point that you can still build your machine even if you don't have the newest – latest. The key is to get the machine up and running with what you have. You can always add components later. In fact, it's guaranteed to happen as you learn more and sharpen your skills. You'll change out power supplies, add more memory, and add more hard drives. This stuff really gets in your blood quickly.

External Storage vs network storage vs internal storage

Here I go again, giving you more pesky choices to make...

Storage is really a matter of cost, convenience and space. One thing to get a clear idea on is that Servers are not like PC's in a LOT of ways. One of those ways has to do with how data can be stored, backed up, retrieved and manipulated differently.

I have one machine that has no hard drives in it at all. It boots to a flash drive that I installed inside the case. The flash drive contains the operating system, several drivers and some instructions that tell the machine what it is when it comes on. The actual data that the machine manipulates is on my main Network Attached Storage (NAS) device. I did it this way because at the time I didn't have the money to buy a bunch of internal storage, but I did have a 3 TB NAS with a bunch of space on it. Since I am just using this machine on my home network and all of the systems are connected to a Gigbit router I get some really fast file transfer speeds between the machines. There will be more on home networks in an upcoming book so stay tuned!

Here's the basic concept. A server (or a computer for that matter) has three alternatives when it comes to storage methods – internal, external, and network.

- **Internal** – this is the most 'basic' method for storage. The hard drive sits inside the case and is physically connected to the motherboard and power via cables. Data is immediately available and you can see the drives by clicking on MY COMPUTER.
- **External** – this method has multiple uses since flash drives have grown so popular, huge in size and cheap. You can configure a flash drive with the operating system or instructions for the machine, mount it to a high speed USB port and instruct the server to boot to the flash drive when it powers on and you're off to the races. This method is really good if you have limited hard drive space and you want to use the internal drives for pure storage. This method also has one very awesome side benefit. Since the operating system is on a flash drive, its easy to make copies to store or replicate your settings to another machine AND (and this is a big bonus) if your main flash drive dies you lose NONE of your data. You just pop one of the copied

flash drives into the machine, tweak a few settings and it's like nothing bad every happened. Believe me when I say that this method is a sanity saver! With high speed USB (*USB 3 is becoming standard and USB 4 is on the way*) you will notice no lag.

- **Network** – this is also an external storage method with a cool twist. With this method you are using not only an external source it also doesn't even have to be in the same room as the server! Earlier I mentioned a Network Attached Storage. It's essentially a hard drive that is physically hard wired to my network and configured in a way that allows me to save and retrieve files from any computer that's attached to it. This also includes my phones, tablets and any other device connected to my network either wired or wireless.

This method is powerful because it allows you to have a central storage location for things like your databases, files, movies, music and even virtual machines. You don't have to store everything on the physical server if you don't want to or don't have space.

The format you choose is up to you, just be aware that the server need not have a hard drive inside it in order to function properly. This opens the door to some seriously creative thinking.

To RAID or not to RAID

I covered RAID a bit earlier in this book and there is a much deeper dive about the concept in a forthcoming For the Tech Hobbyist release, but I thought it would be a good idea to give you a little more information.

You don't necessarily have to use RAID. Your server will work fine without it, but when you consider the potential disaster of losing all of your data and files to a power surge, a failed drive or some other calamity, RAID begins to show its appeal.

RAID offers a method of copying your data across multiple drives making it much more difficult for a single failure to stop you in your tracks. There are hardware methods to create a RAID array involving specialized expansion cards called RAID controllers, and there are software methods built into some motherboards that work just fine (*but are a bit slower than the physical card methods*).

Here are some of the basics –

- RAID has multiple 'levels' each one does something slightly different to protect your data.
- There are multiple different 'levels' of RAID, but I'm only going to talk about the primary ones that you will see/use in your experimenting.
- **RAID 0** splits the data across two or more disks (*known as striping*), but it does not check for parity errors (*if the data is wrong, it gets copied wrong*) and this level has no fault tolerance. What this basically means is, if one drive fails you lose all of your data.   This method is pretty fast though.
- **RAID 1** makes an exact copy of your data on two or more drives (*known as mirroring*) so it's basically a one for one image of the data on two hard drives. This method has no striping and no parity, but if you lose one drive the other still has a viable copy of your data. This one is a little weird because the write and read speeds are limited by the speed of the slowest hard drive. If you have 6 drives and 1 of them runs at 5400 rpm, the read/write speed will be limited to 5400 even if the other drives run faster.   If you're considering RAID make sure you buy drives that run at the same speed (*oh, and they need to be the same size too...*)

- **RAID 5** consists of block-level striping with parity distributed across all of the drives. This is the point at which you need to have 3 or more drives. RAID 5 has a cool ability to rebuild the data from a failed drive when you replace the broken physical one with a new one. This process can be VERY slow, so be aware and have extra drives of the same type on standby. Some companies recommend against using RAID 5 for really important data since the failure of another drive while you're trying to rebuild your array can cost you ALL of your data. Also be aware that despite the power that this level gives by having the data spread out in a way that would allow you to lose almost half of your drives, the read/write using RAID 5 is VERY slow compared to other methods. Personally, I never use this one, it's annoying...
- **RAID 6** this level is pretty much the same as RAID 5, but it adds another parity block across all of the drives, so instead of one parity check you now have two. You won't notice any issues with reading data, but writing data can be slow because it takes a while for the system to do all of the parity calculations (*making sure that the data it receives is the same as the data that was sent*). This level is okay, but I'm not sure I see the benefit for home use.
- **RAID 10** (really RAID 1+0) this level is a combination of RAID 1 and RAID 0 and includes the best of both worlds. This is the method I find myself using more often than not. This one is probably the most 'expensive' of the RAID configurations because it requires a minimum of 4 drives. This level stripes data across mirrored pairs. This of it this way it beaks 4 or 6 or 8 drives into two equal pairs. It then writes the data across both drives in that pair using striping and mirroring. The problem comes in if two of the drives in a single mirrored pair fail at the same time that pair will be unrecoverable and you could potentially lose all of your data. The strength of this

level comes from the number of drives that can fail (so long as they aren't in the same mirrored pair) before you lose any data. Say you have 8 drives; up to 4 of them could fail so long as they aren't in the same set and you'll be fine. It might take forever to rebuild the downed drives, but a little waiting never hurt anyone whereas lost data is VERY painful.

That's RAID in a nutshell. Whether or not you use it is up to you, your needs and how much you want to try to take on. I will admit this, I was building servers for almost 2 years before I finally decided to take the plunge and build one that used RAID 5. It worked and the learning experience was pretty cool, but it added a layer of uncertainty to the project. I'm not saying don't do it, but make sure you have your concepts down pat before you roll down that road.

Section Summary

There is a lot to consider when you're building a server. System uses, cost and availability of components, one part or brand over another, future expansion, and whether or not to use hardware that you have on hand.

Never let that stop you though.

One of the best aspects of building your own system comes from the skills you pick up along the way. Yeah, I mean technical skills, but I'm also talking about 'intangibles' like research skills, planning skills, logistics and project management skills. Things that might not seem super important until you realize that you've gone through a process and came out on the other end with something new that you built with your brain and your own two hands. There's no putting a price on that kind of education and success.

Part 3 – How everything fits together

- Specific component facts
- Building from scratch?
- Repurposing an older machine?
- Section Summary

Component facts

Processors
- The processor is a microchip that contains millions of microscopic circuits
- Every 'computer' has a processor, this includes things like some watches, tablets, cell phones, the systems that run your car, Televisions and lately some appliances
- The processor simply runs numbers all day, calculating instructions received from various sources like applications running in memory, user input, input from connected peripherals and input from outside sources (*the internet comes to mind*)
- Processor performance is measured by its 'clock speed' or how fast it does calculations

Motherboards
- The single point of contact for every other component in a server case
- Also called mainboard, mobo, system board, or logic board
- The motherboard contains slots for expansion cards and RAM modules, and an I/O port for the connection of outside peripherals
- External peripheral ports can include USB 2 & 3, HDMI, fire wire, DisplayPort, audio, and network connections
- Have three 'main' form factors – AT, ATX and microATX
- Use a 'system bus' – a method of connecting the motherboard to every other component in the server –

The bus is designed to pass signals from the component back and forth to the motherboard. The faster this bus operates the faster the overall system will work. There are three main buses – a data bus to carries information, and address bus determines where the information should be sent and the control bus determines the necessary operation.

- Help determine the best case size for your purpose.

Hard Drives (Storage)

- Have a primary purpose of providing non-volatile storage of data (*data doesn't go away when the power is turned off*).
- Are either older spinning platter type, or solid state device type machines.
- Can be internal, external or even network devices.
- Have been around and getting smaller physically while increasing in storage space since 1963.
- Every device designed to store data has some kind of hard drive in it (or IS a hard drive with other technology wrapped around it).
- Can be set up to work in tandem with other hard drives logically increasing the total storage space you have to work with.

Memory (RAM)

- The acronym RAM stands for **R**andom **A**ccess **M**emory which means the data stored on the chip while it's active can be accessed in a random fashion. The processor doesn't have to seek information sequentially which speeds things up.
- It's important not to skimp on RAM, this is where the OS and many device drivers load when the server starts, it's also where the processor gets all of the information that it needs and if the RAM is sketchy you're going to have all kinds of strange problems.
- More RAM is always better than not enough, you'll find that most applications have a 'minimum' RAM to function well, when you do your research make sure

you take note and get the most RAM for your money. If you have a limited budget (and who doesn't lately...) you can buy enough to get you started and then buy more later on when you have a chance.
- Unlike hard drives RAM is dependent on a clean supply of electricity; if you lose power whatever was held in RAM is gone. It's also much more susceptible to being damaged by power spikes.

Power Supply
- Supplies power to every component within the case via cable or direct physical connection.
- Better quality power supplies will help keep your server cooler and provide it with cleaner power.
- Only buy a power supply rated over 750 Watts if your server is specifically going to use that level of power, probably 90% of your machines never will.
- Power supplies convert AC power to DC power of various voltages and amperages since the motherboard provides different amounts of power to different components.

Case
- Whether aesthetic or functional your case is what the world see's when they look at your server. Depending on what type of machine your building or where it's going to be housed the case will only matter for its function.
- Cases come in several shapes known as form factors
  - Tower – a lot like the shape of your typical PC. They can be somewhat larger to accommodate more hard drives and larger motherboards.
  - Rack mount – a flat chassis that is intended to be mounted in a server rack or cage
  - ATX – usually a small form factor case meant for sitting on or under a desk, these cases are usually much smaller than a typical PC

- o Cube – cool shape that's good for devices that will be in the public eye or if you have limited space.
- The case usually contains all of the server components, but that sometimes isn't feasible. When space is at a premium and the server will not feature internal storage or even a hard drive to hold the operating system flash drives can be used for that function. There are several operating systems that do not care where they are installed so long as they can start and access resources where needed. This opens up a bit of flexibility for you. If cost is an initial concern and the server you're building will pull its files from some other source (an external NAS, a network resource, a USB connected flash drive or even another server) then a smaller form factor fits the bill.
- The case is designed to help cool the components stored inside of it and to protect them from dust and the elements. They are usually made of aluminum although some serious creative experimenters have created cases of plexiglass, plastic, rubber and even wood. Honestly it's all up to your imagination.

Okay so those are all the basic component facts. I recommend that you spend some time researching anything that's still not clear. I'm trying not to leave anything out where the basics are concerned but I'm sure I'll miss one or two things. One thing to know about working with technology in general and servers specifically, methods tend to change regularly as new components are offered to the market.
It's VERY important that you keep yourself updated.

If you're building from scratch

Well alright then!

You've decided to take on the challenge of building something that's never existed before. That's great news! You'll be able to do this project from start to finish much faster than you might think and the sense of pride you'll get from the finished project will be all yours to bask in.

Having said that I'm going to go out on a limb here and pre-suppose that you're building this server for more than just the adulation of your adoring fans. It's my guess that you really want to build something functional with a daily use in mind.

In the first FTTH book I talked about the reasons why you'd want to build a server in the first place and I listed several types of servers that would be fairly easy to build which would provide you with a useful service.

Here are the 10 most popular uses of home servers –

- File & Print
- Streaming audio and video files to your TV's or other devices
- Controlling house functions (lights, heating/cooling, timers, locks, alarms, cameras, etc)
- Gaming
- Storing data or acting as a central location for backing up home PCs
- Creating a virtual lab for certification studies
- VPN services for secure remote access
- Controlling access to your home network using DNS and DHCP
- TV portal for watching streaming video feeds
- Home web server

This list isn't exhaustive. There are other purposes for a home server, but the 10 listed above are the most prevalent uses.

Building your machine from scratch really puts what you want the server to do into perspective. You will be purchasing your components with one or two very specific purpose in mind. This will help keep you focused and also help cut down on unnecessary purchases.

Along with considering what type server to build it's a good idea to ask yourself some follow-up questions, like –

- How many hours per day do you think you will use the server? (Some machines are 24/7 and some are only on when you need them.)
- How many people will access the server on a daily basis?
- Will the server need to be connected to the internet so you can access it remotely? (And if so, how will you handle remote access?)
- Do you have lots of audio, video and movie files to store or stream?
- Where will the server live in your home?
- What kind of budget are you working with?
  - Will you have to buy parts over the course of a few weeks or months or can you plan out and get everything at one time? This can make a difference because prices for components can change pretty rapidly.
- What operating system will you be using? (There will be more on OS's in the third book of this series.)

I'm sure that as you become more skilled at building servers you will answer some questions much quicker and find new ones to ask along the way. It's all a learning process which is part of what makes it so fun.

If you are going to repurpose

Re-purposing an older machine to turn it into a server is obviously the easier of the two methods, but while it has its strengths it also has some serious drawbacks.

On the good side –

- You don't have to buy anything (or very little).
- You already know the hardware. You know how fast it is, how big the hard drive is and so forth.
- You probably have parts lying around to do functional upgrades if necessary, again saving money and time.
- The machine may already have an operating system on it that will work just fine as a converted server. Windows 7 has some features in it that definitely make this possible. (Printer sharing and media streaming leap quickly to mind.

And then there's the bad stuff –

- The memory, processor and storage might be inadequate or so antiquated as to be useless.
- The machine may be too old to upgrade readily. Finding parts for machines as recent as 5 years ago can be a chore. 5 years in computerland is like a 100 years in real life. Anyone remember RAMBUS memory? No? Moving on...
- The network interface in the machine might be too slow for fast data transfers. It wasn't all that long ago that most Network Interface Cards had a top speed of only 10 MBps. With today's file sizes starting in the gigabyte range, the time it takes to transfer a single file might make you want to tear your hair out.
(Also, just as a side note, the speed I'm talking about is for file transfers within your own network. The speed of you NIC has very little to do with the speed of the internet your ISP is providing you.)

- If the machine has 32 bit architecture you might be severely limited to what it can do. That's not to say that 32 bit machines should be trashed. Far from it. There are a ton of things they can be used for. They just won't run some higher end software and they're usually not as fast.

There are two sides to every coin, but at the end of the day remember this – all coins spend the same. You can build a machine from scratch or you can find a use for an older machine, either way works.

Section Summary

You've got some interesting times ahead. My experience taught me that planning and building a server can be more fun than maintaining the finished product. I think that's what spurs me to build better systems.

I am solidly on the fence about whether to build from scratch or re-use a system you already own. I've done both with good and bad results. One of my oldest machines was meant to run Windows 95. It took a while to find a version of Linux that would run on the machine only to discover that it barely had enough memory to run one application. I didn't toss it, I just turned it into a device that sits just behind my home router and monitors traffic in and out of my network.

There were several times that I wanted to give up on that project, but I'm glad now that I didn't. I learned a lot and the machine has been awesome at its job. I wouldn't want it any other way. Yes it's old and will eventually die, but that's okay. I'll just build something else, that's the nature of this particular hobby.

Good Luck!

Authors Note:

We hope you find this book series useful and easy to follow. This series is intended to help the technology fan build their knowledge base with information on a wide range of topics. This first book is all about giving you a basic idea of what a server is what they can do and most importantly to spark the creative drive in you to build your own!

The rest of the books in the 'Everything you want to know about Home Severs' series cover some ways to acquire the parts to build a server, the actual construction, installing and configuring operating systems and whatever other goodies we can think to throw in.

If this book series got your creative juices flowing please consider the other books in the For the Tech Hobbyist series. They include guides on –

- Raspberry Pi
- Ubuntu Linux fun stuff
- Mass storage devices
- Virtualization for the home network
- Home automation
- FreeNAS fun stuff
- OwnCloud – your private storage box
- Fighting viruses on your home PC's
- Home security systems

And many more to come!

www.ingramcontent.com/pod-product-compliance
Lightning Source LLC
Chambersburg PA
CBHW071553080326
40690CB00056B/1994